RED FOXES

Published by Smart Apple Media
1980 Lookout Drive, North Mankato, MN 56003

Design and Production by The Design Lab/Kathy Petelinsek

Photographs by Patrick Endres, Robert McCaw, Joe McDonald,
Mary Ann McDonald, Tom Stack & Associates (Erwin & Peggy Bauer,
Lynn Gerig, Victoria Hurst, Thomas Kitchin, Spencer Swanger)

Library of Congress Cataloging-in-Publication Data
Whitledge, Doran.
Red Foxes / by Doran and Jane Whitledge.
p. cm. — (Northern trek)
ISBN 1-58340-070-2
1. Red Fox—Juvenile literature. [1. Red Fox. 2. Foxes.] I. Whitledge, Jane. II. Title. III. Series.

QL737.C22 W52   2001
599.775—dc21   00-050489

First Edition

2   4   6   8   9   7   5   3   1

NORTHERN TREK

RED FOXES

WRITTEN BY DORAN AND JANE WHITLEDGE

SMART APPLE MEDIA

In the fading light of evening, the red fox roams the woodlands and meadows of rural North America. Throughout the night and into the growing morning light, this wild member of the dog family most actively pursues its life as a hunter. Catlike in its quickness and night vision, the red fox claims the woods and fields while most humans sleep. Even though this wild hunter is sought by trappers for its fur, hunted with hounds for sport, and persecuted by farmers, it has slowly increased its numbers and spread into new territories.

A SHY PREDATOR, the red fox (*Vulpes vulpes*) favors the mixed landscape of farm fields, woodlots, and country roadsides that characterizes much of North America. The red fox is smart and secretive, and so well adapted to a world dominated by human developments that it is one of the most widespread of the world's **terrestrial** predators. It is found not only throughout most of North America, but in Europe, Asia, and Africa as well. It has been introduced into Australia and has become abundant there.

The red fox is the smallest member of the dog family. Standing about 16 inches (40 cm) high at the shoulder, it has a bushy tail that may be half or more of the fox's total length. The red fox's color may vary—some are gray or black—but most are a reddish color, with black legs, ears, and muzzles. Foxes also have white on their throats and tail tips and the undersides of their faces and bellies.

The fox has many names around the world. It is called "Tod" in England, "Renard" in France, and "Lisa" in Russia.

The red fox is small, lightweight, and quick. This makes it well suited to hunt mice, insects, **reptiles**, **amphibians**, and birds. Using its sensitive hearing, the fox can locate mice that are hidden from sight under leaves, grass, and even snow. By listening carefully, it learns where the hidden mouse is, then pounces on the spot.

The fox also hunts larger prey, such as grouse, pheasants, rabbits, and squirrels. To catch these, it must sneak close and make a surprise rush. The fox resembles a cat in the way it **stalks** its **prey**. The fox is also a scavenger. If a larger predator has killed a deer or moose, the fox will

The fox can survive the winter on mostly berries and seeds, but it eats best during the summer, when prey—such as squirrels and birds—is plentiful.

Rural foxes eat about 50 percent mice, voles, and other small rodents and only about 6 percent trash and discarded human food. Foxes near cities, however, eat only 30 percent small prey and up to 25 percent trash and discarded food.

take some of the meat if it can. If the fox has more meat than it can eat, it buries the excess to eat later.

Protecting food supplies is especially important in late winter, when red foxes mate. At this time of year, the countryside acquires the smell of foxes' scent markings. Scent marks are small deposits of strong-smelling urine that foxes leave to mark their territories so that other foxes will stay out.

The fox's senses of hearing and smell are so acute that it can even detect prey hiding under heavy snow.

Some foxes may fall prey to their larger cousins, wolves and coyotes. When a fox is attacked by these bigger and stronger predators, its only chance of survival is to outrun them.

By claiming their own exclusive territory, a mated fox pair can keep other foxes from taking the prey they'll need for themselves and their young. Keeping other foxes out of their territory also protects the mated pair's young from other foxes. The territorial needs of mating foxes help keep the land from becoming overcrowded with foxes, since these animals won't mate unless they have room to mark out their own territory.

Fox pups (also called kits) are born in the early spring. Foxes usually have four to seven pups, which are born in a tunnel that the mother digs. Foxes don't otherwise live in dens—they sleep in the open. The den is a place where the **vulnerable** young pups can have some protection from the many things that threaten them—everything from bad weather to bird and animal predators that prey on young foxes.

At first, the mother fox, or vixen, stays in the den with the new pups. She keeps the pups warm and nurses them. In their first weeks of life, the pups are fed only their mother's milk. They grow rapidly.

Soon the mother fox can leave the pups alone in the den while she goes out to hunt. She returns at intervals to nurse the pups, to keep them clean, and to feed them whatever meat she can catch. The male, or dog fox, also brings in mice, birds, snakes, squirrels, rabbits, or whatever he can

Only the highest-ranking vixens are allowed to breed, assuring that healthy pups will be added to the family groups.

find. By early summer the young foxes eat only meat and wild fruits.

As the young foxes grow, they spend more and more time outside their den. Summer is a time of growth and learning for them. Through playful wrestling and tumbling, they learn the fighting skills they'll need to defend themselves and their own territories when they become adults. By stalking each other and pouncing on grasshoppers, they learn the first lessons of a hunter's life.

Their parents take them on short hunting trips, but most of the time the growing pups play or rest near the den. Even when they're old enough to wander away on their own hunts, the fox pups will return to spend time at the den.

Pups fight each other to determine their level of dominance and respect in the family group. The outcome of such fights establishes how each fox will be treated for the rest of its life.

By autumn, the fox pups, able to care for themselves, spend little time at the den. In the relative safety of the family territory, they have learned the things they need to know. As grown foxes, they will move out to find territories of their own. The young males will be the first to go, hurried on their way by their father, who doesn't want male competitors in his territory.

The grown vixen pups may stay on to help their parents raise next year's litter. These vixens may, in another year, mate with male foxes in different territories and raise their own pups. Foxes may travel far to find new territories, and they can easily adapt to a variety of habitats.

The red fox has been native to North America for at least 14,000 years. Early American

colonists, wanting red foxes to hunt for sport, brought some from England. These imported foxes bred with the native North American foxes and spread to fill the land in greater numbers.

Today, the red fox is more widespread than ever before. While foxes are still hunted for sport or for their **pelts**, or because they disturb farm animals, these fascinating creatures continue to prosper around the world. This is largely due to the fragmented landscape of fields, woodlots, and roadside ditches that humans have created—and that foxes have adopted as home.

Foxes are good travelers and can cover a lot of ground in a short time when they need to. Some foxes make trails that they use over and over again, marking them with urine or scat.

THE RED FOX, though widespread, is secretive and is not numerous anywhere. The best place to see one is a zoo, though watching fields and roadsides during the morning and evening may eventually offer you a glimpse of a fox. The fact that it isn't easy will make the sighting more special.

The surest way to see a wild fox is to watch an active den from a tree or a remote hiding place. Foxes live in many parks and wildlife refuges. Call one near you to see if foxes have been seen there. As you would on any trek into nature, remember that wild animals are unpredictable and can be dangerous if approached. The best way to view wildlife is from a respectful—and safe—distance.

ROCKY MOUNTAIN NATIONAL PARK IN COLORADO *With more than 100 peaks towering over 11,000 feet (3,353 m), this park has road access from the lower parts of the park to the higher. Among the many animals in this beautiful park are red foxes.*

MUSCATATUCK NATIONAL WILDLIFE REFUGE IN INDIANA *This diverse 7,724-acre (3,126 h) refuge has a wide variety of wildlife, among which is the red fox. Fox sightings are also possible in nearby state parks.*

AFTON STATE PARK IN MINNESOTA *This park near the St. Croix River has 3,000 acres (1,214 h) and 20 miles (32 km) of trails. Red foxes are occasionally seen crossing roads and open fields, or at the edges of clearings.*

SLEEPING GIANT PROVINCIAL PARK IN ONTARIO *Part of the Sibley Peninsula, this stunning park arcs 22 miles (35 km) into Lake Superior. The landscape is a mix of woods, hills, and shoreline, and there are several fine vantage points from which to view the lake. Foxes live in the park, as well as moose and many other smaller animals.*

amphibians: *smooth-skinned, cold-blooded animals that spend part of their lives underwater, including frogs, toads, and salamanders*

pelts: *the furry skins of animals*

predator: *an animal that kills other animals for food*

prey: *an animal hunted for food by a predator*

reptiles: *scaly-skinned, cold-blooded animals, including snakes, lizards, and turtles*

stalks: *sneaks up on*

terrestrial: *taking place on land*

vulnerable: *without defense*